Blogging Business:

How to start a blog that is a Business.

Table of Contents

Introduction

Chapter One: Blogging as Passive Income

Chapter Two: Choosing a Niche to Blog About

Chapter Three: Choosing a Host Site

Chapter Four: Creating a Blog with WordPress

Chapter Five: Publishing Schedules

Chapter Six: Monetizing Your Blog

Chapter Seven: Promoting Your Blog

Chapter Eight: Social Media and Blogging

Chapter Nine: Email Marketing

Chapter Ten: Blogging Tips

Conclusion

© Copyright 2016 - All rights reserved.

The follow eBook is reproduced below with the goal of providing information that is as accurate and reliable as possible. Regardless, purchasing this Book can be seen as consent to the fact that both the publisher and the author of this book are in no way experts on the topics discussed within and that any recommendations or suggestions that are made herein are for entertainment purposes only. Professionals should be consulted as needed prior to undertaking any of the action endorsed herein.

This declaration is deemed fair and valid by both the American Bar Association and the Committee of Publishers Association and is legally binding throughout the United States.

Furthermore, the transmission, duplication or reproduction of any of the following work including specific information will be considered an illegal act irrespective of if it is done electronically or in print. This extends to creating a secondary or tertiary copy of the work or a recorded copy and is only allowed with express written consent from the Publisher. All additional right reserved.

The information in the following pages is broadly considered to be a truthful and accurate account of facts and as such any inattention, use or misuse of the information in question by the reader will render any resulting actions solely under their purview. There are no scenarios in which the publisher or the original author of this work can be in any fashion deemed liable for any hardship or damages that may befall them after undertaking information described herein.

Additionally, the information in the following pages is intended only for informational purposes and should thus be thought of as universal. As befitting its nature, it is presented without assurance regarding its prolonged validity or interim quality. Trademarks that are mentioned are done without written consent and can in no way be considered an endorsement from the trademark holder.

Introduction

Congratulations on downloading *Blogging Business from Home* and thank you for doing so.

The following chapters will discuss how you can turn a blog into your very own business, generating passive income and creating a stay-at-home business in the process. You may even find that you may be able to quit your day job and stay at home full-time writing for your blog if that is something that you want to do.

Everyone knows what a blog is, but do you really know the benefits that come from having a blog as a business? Do you understand what you need to know so that you can make a profit from your blog? Inside the pages of this book, you are going to discover all that you need to know to start your own blogging business from home.

There are plenty of books on this subject on the market, thanks again for choosing this one! Every effort was made to ensure it is full of as much useful information as possible; please enjoy!

Chapter One: Blogging as Passive Income

With the traditional 9-to-5 job fast becoming a thing of the past, taking with it things like job security and long term benefits, there are few in the workforce these days that could not benefit from an extra income stream. Passive income opportunities such as blogging provide you with just that, a type of income stream that isn't directly related to the hours you put in each day. While this doesn't mean that you won't ever have to put any work into getting your blog up and running, what it does mean is that once you are established you can be bringing in a much more than you would with the same amount of effort from a traditional job.

One way that you can earn money passively is through the blog posts that you have already created. Writing the actual post is going to be considered active income, but after that post has moved into your archives, it still can earn you money. You may be surprised to find that some of your more popular posts are actually in your archives and are still going to make you money well into the future. As long as you monetize your site properly and generate evergreen content then you can generate years of revenue from hours, or even minutes, of work.

Whenever you allow an ad from a network such as AdSense you are going to be enabling ad publishers to place pieces of their code into your blog that way they can run ads automatically for a predetermined period of time. Setting up the most common types of advertising deals will allow you to decide broadly where your advertisements will go before letting the advertising network that you are working with decide what types of ads go where specifically. These ads then bring in a small but steady passive income stream without you having to do anything but continue generating content as normal.

Benefits of passive income

Bosses: When you are a blogger, you are going to be your own boss. You are not going to be held responsible by anyone else when you decide to sit around watching YouTube videos all day instead of doing any actual work. This benefit is a double-edged sword, however because it also means that there will be nobody looking over your shoulder forcing you to work when there is work that needs to be done. If you are someone who appreciates the structure of a traditional office environment, then you may want to think long and hard about your personal motivation levels before making the switch if you want things to go as smoothly as possible.

Endless variety: Rather than working in an office day in and day out, no two days working as a blogger are ever going to be the same. By necessity you are always going to be researching new topics, which you are hopefully interested in, and if you get bored and want to take things in a completely different direction, well that's completely up to you. The only person you are accountable to is your readership, otherwise the sky is the limit. If you are looking for a reliable job where you don't have to make a lot of choices, you might want to look elsewhere.

You'll see more of your money: As an employee of a major company, the amount that you make each month is going to be a far cry from the amount that you actually take home at the end of the day. With state and federal taxes, plus health insurance and who knows what else, many employees are only taking home about 70 percent of their total pay, if they are lucky. As a blogger, on the other hand, you work for yourself which means that when you earn $20 from an advertiser as a commission for helping them sell a product, that $20 doesn't go anywhere but into your pocket. While the same amount, if not more, will ultimately go out when everything is said and done, the fact of the matter is that you are going to be more in charge of your overall destiny as a blogger and that fact is extremely appealing to some people.

Portability: A majority of jobs only offer a couple of weeks off a year for vacations because they do not want work production to decrease while you are gone. Working from home blogging is going to empower you to travel wherever you want to go whenever you want to! A major plus with vacations from your own passive income job is that you are not going to have to work if you do not want to. But, if you choose to, all you have to do is pop open your laptop and connect to the internet!

As with vacations, you are going to be free to take your job with you whenever you want to. If you have to travel because of a spouse's job or because you want to go see family, your work can be in the car with you as you travel across the state or country. On top of that, you can change your scenery when you feel cooped up in your house. The only true limiting factors are electricity and an internet connection, and if you are truly taking to the road both of these can be taken with you as well. The same things most certainly cannot be said for an office.

No coworkers: Dealing with office politics is an unfortunate part of most jobs. When you are working for yourself as a blogger, however, you don't need to worry about accidentally stepping on the wrong toes because you won't have anyone to bother you except for people you live with. While a life without coworkers might seem nice, it is important to understand that blogging can also be an isolating profession. If you are a naturally social person you might want to give it a try before you commit full time.

Irregular schedule: Most jobs have a set schedule as well as a clear delineation as to when the employee is working and not working. As a blogger, you never have to work if you don't want to, but at the same time you are never really not working. Weekends are when you will find lots of traffic and if an ad on your site breaks you are going to need to do everything you can to fix it regardless if it is 2 pm or 2 am. If you like the idea of working in smaller chunks as opposed to 8 hour bursts, then blogging might be the job for you.

Job security: While most jobs have many benefits, the fact of the matter is that one area where they are lacking is when it comes to true job security. With few exceptions, working for a major company means that you have very little control over whether you would still have a job tomorrow if someone higher up the ladder said so. Working for yourself is somewhat of an interesting dichotomy in that you absolutely cannot be fired, yet at the same time your job is tenuous because if you lose your audience you have nothing. As each side of the coin certainly has its benefits, deciding which is better is really a personal choice.

Pursue your passion: For many people, the job that they go to every day is simply a means to an end in that it lets them pursue their passions on their off hours. The best blogs are about people sharing their passions, however, which means that most bloggers eat, sleep and breath that which they are most passionate about. The old adage about work and doing what you love is true, if you can merge them then you can really feel as though you never work a day in your life. It is important that you chose an aspect of the passion that can be varied and provides you with plenty of options to appreciate it from all sides, otherwise you might regret you ever started.

Alternative to traditional retirement options: As previously mentioned, when it comes to planning for retirement, there are few better ways of doing so these days than via the type of passive income that will be generated after you get your blog up and running. While it won't quite be the completely worry and work free life that those who retired 20 years ago might have had, it is still going to be a fair bit more laid back than those who didn't prepare with their own passive income plans. What's more, unlike many retirement plans, yours will remain completely in your own hands which means you won't have to worry about anyone else making decisions that have the potential to seriously alter the quality of your life.

Chapter Two: Choosing a Niche to Blog About

Once you have decided that blogging is the right type of passive income stream for you, the next thing that you will need to do is choose a niche that you will eventually start blogging about. Choosing the right niche to blog about is difficult because you want to choose something that you are passionate about, yet something that is no so well covered that it will be impossible for you to find an audience. Additionally, you are going to want to ensure that it is something that is popular enough that it has its own unique audience. This audience is the niche that you are seeking and if you manage to find the right one then it makes building your blog, and eventually all of your brand, that much easier.

While finding a niche that is the right mix of popular but underserved might seem difficult at first, the ease with which you pick up readers who are disenfranchised from more broader topics will make all of it more than worthwhile in the long run as these are the individuals that will make your blog profitable. Furthermore, when it comes to picking the right topic you are going to want to ensure that not only are there plenty of disenfranchised individuals floating around who are interested in the topic, but that they are willing to spend money on their interest as well.

Choosing a topic and generating an audience won't do you any good if the audience you find isn't interested in spending money on their interest or if the items that they do buy are exceedingly cheap. Finding the right mix of enthusiasm and disposable income can be difficult, but once you tap into the right market you will be able to confidentially approach advertisers knowing that you have something they desperately want. This is why choosing the right topic is something that requires more than a few minutes of thought, it requires dedicated research.

Choosing the right topic

Choosing a blogging topic that is based on popularity is not a bad idea. However, the more popular the topic that you choose, the more people are going to have a blog dedicated to that topic thus making you have more competition.

Popularity is not going to be everything. Look at what people read when they are not online as well as what they read when they are online. Being able to answer any questions that people may have about a particular topic is going to assist you in choosing the proper topic.

Once you have created a list of things that you have found that people are reading online and offline, you have completed step one of finding the right topic. This list is going to direct you in finding a topic that is going to be read by people as well as not have a lot of competition like a blog about a popular celebrity might.

Favorite blogs

When you are online doing your research, you can go to your search engine and type in popular blogs and you are going to have the ability see all the blogs that are trending.

Choose several of these blogs and look at the topics that they write about and the different things that they do to attract readers. Take note of these strategies because you are going to be able to use them, but do not copy them exactly. You are going to want your blog to be your own and not a copy of someone else's hard work.

Popular books

Just like you did with the blogs, you need to have some of the books that people are reading on your list. To find the books that are popular, you should go to websites like Amazon and Barnes and Nobel to look at the best sellers list.

A lot of these best sellers are going to be by authors that are popular, but that is why people are reading them. You should not create a website about the author because that most likely has already been done, however, knowing what the book is about will help you when it comes to choosing a topic that is going to be read by readers all over the world.

Pursue Problems and Concerns

Everyone has questions about the things of life. It goes to stand that if you can create a blog that is going to not only answer these questions, but maybe even challenge the way that people think, you are going to have a truly successful blog.

To add to the list that you have already created that have potential topics to write about, put some of the questions that people are asking. If you can answer these questions with the proper research, then you are one step closer to perhaps having a blog that no one else has started.

You are going to have to do research of course to make sure that you are providing the correct information and not putting out posts that are not containing the truth. If they cannot be checked, then you are going to lose readers. So, should you decide to make your blog about any questions or concerns that people are having, ensure that you are picking topics that you can write about properly.

Choosing a profitable niche

You want your blog to succeed and in order to do that, you have to look at the list of topics that you have created and pick something that is not only unique, but something that you are going to be able to write a blog on.

You are not going to have all of your posts about the topic that you have chosen, but you should be prepared to create enough posts on the topic that you pick to be sure that your readers are fully informed.

Before you settle on a topic, you should also pull up your search engine and type in keywords that have to do with that topic to scope out any competition you may have.

Choosing the right keywords and phrases: Once you have a good idea for a general topic, the next thing that you will want to do is to determine the phrases and words that are most commonly associated with it. These are the words that are going to be used in various search engines when people are looking for the topic in question. If you are very familiar with the topic then you can likely brainstorm a list yourself, otherwise visiting websites that you are familiar with in the general niche and then right-clicking on the page will allow you to access the source code for the site where any tagged words and phrases will be hiding.

After you have a good list of words and phrases that relate to the niche you are considering the next thing you will need to do is to is plug each into your search engine of choice and see how many different sources come up. If you see the same handful of sites time and again then you might want to start over as competition is going to be fierce. The more variety you see when you punch in your keywords of choice the better, this means the audience for the topic is divided and may still look favorably on a new blog in the space.

Consider sub-niches: If you find that the niche you were planning on really digging into seems to be a little bit more full than you would otherwise like, there is no need to abandon it completely. Instead you just need to drill down into it more thoroughly and find a section of the market that is still not being represented. While not every niche is going to be large enough to have subsections of an audience, you will be surprised how people categorize themselves when given the chance.

Ensure you aren't making a huge mistake: Finally, once you have a clear idea of what your niche is going to be, you are going to want to take what you have found and look into the various sites that you will be competing against. Just because these sites aren't major enough to control all of the top slots on the search engine results doesn't mean they aren't major enough to make it difficult for you to find advertisers who aren't having their needs met elsewhere. To ensure you are up to the task you are going to want to watch the competition for a few weeks to determine if you can keep up with their output and content. If you find that you can't don't get discouraged and instead be grateful that you didn't waste any more time on an idea that ultimate would not have panned out.

Before you start, you should be certain that you are picking the topic that you are going to be able to write about properly. Go through all the steps once again and see if there is anything better that you could write about. If there is something else that you are going to be able to write better based on the steps that are listed above, then you should choose that topic.

Competition is not a bad thing and it does not matter what topic you pick; you are going to have some sort of competition. The biggest thing is to pick a topic that is going to bring you less competition so that you are able to pull out on top and become the best blog that there is on the topic that you pick to write about.

Chapter Three: Choosing a Host Site

With a niche and possibly a sub-niche chosen, you are finally on your way to running a successful blogging business from home. The next thing that you are going to need to do is build a website which means starting by choosing a hosting company. This is the company that will be in charge of ensuring your site stays online with minimal interference and it is important to be very choosy when picking the one that is best for you.

Host site considerations

Cost: Price is important to anyone. When you are looking at possible host sites, you should review the services that they are going to offer you and find the one that is in your price range, not only now, but after the introductory year of rates is up as well. You should easily be able to find a hosting company that charges less than $10 per month, less than $5 for the first year if you pay in full. It is important to not put cost before everything else, however, as doing so can easily leave you stuck in a contract with inferior service. As such, it is important to read plenty of reviews before making your ultimate decision.

Data transfer limits: It is imperative to look at how much data you are going to be able to move through your blog every month when you are looking at hosting companies. Many seemingly great deals have transfer limits, and your limit needs to be set high so that it is able to accommodate all of the data that may be published in a month. Everything that you publish is going to be viewed be every single person that visits your blog which means that while you might not be concerned about any potential caps early on, eventually they could become very important which is why you need to pay attention to them from the start.

Space: Much like with transfer limits, space is likely not something that you will need to concern yourself with initially, though it could become a problem eventually if you are too limited in your options down the line. If your site is primarily going to be text based then you will not need to worry much about space, though if you are taking lots of high quality pictures then you may want to consider purchasing some additional space. Regardless, a terabyte of space is going to be more than enough storage for any blogger who is not posting gigabytes and gigabytes of video onto their blog.

Reliability: Especially in the early days, if your readers are not able to get on your site and see what you have posted on a regular basis, or if server issues prevent you from posting for a prolonged period of time, then they are going to leave and never come back. This means it is vital to choose a host company that has a reliability of at least 99.5 percent. Anything else is simply not worth the risk.

Also, if the speed of accessing your site is slow because the host's server has exceeded the capacity, then your readers are going to get frustrated and just exit your blog rather than waiting for your site to load. Evaluate the host's reliability so that you are sure that your visitors are going to be able to get into your site and you are getting what you are paying for.

Support: Prior to pulling the trigger on any hosting site, it is important that you make it a point to determine how easy they are to get a hold of. The only time you will ever need to speak with your hosting company is if you are in the middle of an emergency which means you are going to need to know that they will be there when you need them. Avoid any company that only offers email access and look for multiple phone numbers as well as close to 24-hour customer service as possible or run the risk of being left out in the cold when it matters most.

Popular hosting sites

eHost: eHost.com is going to provide you with a free domain for the lifetime of your plan at the cost of $2.75 per month, per year that you purchase in bulk. They also provide access to a custom HTML site builder for those who know how to code. They also provide 24-hour customer services as well as access to the common cPannel website management system. They also offer a money back guarantee for 45 days so there is very little risk for those who are on the fence about the service.

iPage: iPage lets you get started for just $2 and comes with a free domain name as well as an email address which is associated with the domain as well. They also offer 24-hour a day support and a 30-day money back guarantee.

HostCle@r: HostCle@r offers a simple web hosting solution for just $2.99 for the first year when it is purchased all at once. It also provides the ability to build a website with drag and drop options as well as a money back guarantee if you are not happy with their services. They also offer 24-hour a day support and a guaranteed level of high server reliability.

Domain names
After you have gone ahead and found a hosting site, it is important that you register the domain name that you are interested in as well. While some sites will let you start a free blog, purchasing your own domain is almost always going to be the right choice. When it comes to choosing a domain name, the most obvious choice is to go with the full name of the blog. If the name of your blog is rather long or is otherwise not available, then you will want to choose something that those in your target niche or sub-niche will relate to specifically. A breakdown of the advantages and disadvantages of owning your own domain name can be found below to ensure you know what you are getting into before you pull the trigger.

Advantages

Professionalism: Having your own domain name is going to give you the advantage of having a website that your website is not going to look like all the other websites that you visit. You are going to have the creative freedom to make your site your own.

In doing this, you are going to be able to hide the fact that you may be new to writing a blog and show that you are serious about what you are doing. Also, with your own domain, you are going to have access to more designs that other bloggers may not have access to since they are using a free version of the site.

Paying for your own domain is going to make it to where you are not stuck with plan designs that are used on almost every blog.

Real Email Address

Owning your domain name is going to enable you to have an email address that is personalized to you and that people are going to be able to recognize as you instead of spam.

When you are using your personal email address, it reflects pieces of your life. It can state that you are a parent, your anniversary date, a pet's name, any number of things that make it personal to you. But, along with that, it also comes from a generic web server such as Google or Yahoo.

These emails tend to get deleted by people because they do not know who the email is coming from and they do not want to put a virus on their computer. However, if your email is coming from an email such as your name and then your domain name's server, people will know that it does not contain anything that is going to harm their computer.

SEO

When people get online and do a search, thousands if not millions of results are returned for what they have searched for. But, when you have your own domain name, it is going to increase the chances of people finding your website.

This is going to be a huge advantage for you when you are trying to get more readers because they are going to see your site first and are most likely going to click on it to see if it is what they are looking for.

Ubiquity

A lot of people only have on website with one suffix. But, when you buy your own domain, you can get multiple domains so that you are spread out across the web. Doing this is going to tie into your SEO so that you are found in more searches.

Not only are you going to be allowed a .com, but you can have sites like .org, .net, .co and many others.

Disadvantages

Cost

There are costs involved in owning your own domain such as paying to keep that domain yours. Then, there are going to be the costs that you have to pay for so that you can keep up the maintenance on your site. The costs may not be very much, but they are going to be fees that you will have to plan into your blogging budget so that you make sure to pay them so that you do not lose your site.

Technical

Creating your own website means that you are starting it from scratch. There are going to be more technical things that you have to set up. You are not only creating your own design, but you are setting up daily sweeps for viruses on your website, as well as the various plug ins that you may want on your site to make it easier for your readers when they want to share something from your site.

Backups

Websites crash all the time. When a website crashes, there is the risk of losing everything that was saved on the website. Losing everything will result in posts that readers were previously saving to look at later no longer being available to them thus causing them an inconvenience and possibly causing them to find another blog to read.

To prevent this from happening, you are going to have to create backups of everything that you post so that in the event that your site crashes, you do not lose everything. Having your own domain means that you have to create your own backups instead of the website that you are using creating them for you.

Most backups are going to be saved on a server, but a good rule of thumb is to keep all of your posts saved to your own personal computer and possibly even offline so that you have multiple copies of them and that you do not lose them.

Chapter Four: Creating a Blog with WordPress

WordPress is one of the most popular websites used when creating a blog. If you do not have a webhost of your own, then WordPress is free. However, you can also have your own domain with WordPress so that the site is completely made by you from scratch.

WordPress Hosted Blog

Step one: creating a blog is the whole reason as to why you are looking at WordPress. With WordPress you are going to be able to share your content online without having to worry about coding and hosting to ensure that your content is being seen by people. All you have to do is upload your content and WordPress will take care of the rest.

But, the ads that are posted on your site, you are not going to earn any money from. These ads are going to give all of the money to WordPress because they are the ones who are making sure that your site is running the way that it is supposed to be.

Step two: start your account. Just like with any other website, the email that you use has to be a valid email before you are able to create a username, password, and the URL for your blog. With the free version of WordPress you are going to have a generic URL that looks like this: Yourwebsitesname.wordpress.com.

If you want a website that is on a .net, .com, or .org, you are going to have to pay a yearly fee to obtain this suffix.

Step three: decide on what settings you want on your blog. On your dashboard, you are going to have the ability to take control of our blog so that you can create the perfect look and feel for how you want it to be set up.

You will want to select the title for your blog so that it appears in the browser whenever someone clicks on your blog. If you change the title it is not going to change the address of your blog.

The tagline will give the reader a short description of what they can expect from your blog. Depending on which theme you decide to go with for the blog, your tagline can either fall below the blog's title, or it will be listed in the title bar.

Your email that you associate with the blog is going to be where all of your emails will go whenever you receive new comments or something has gone wrong with your blog that you need to know about.

The time zone that you select for your blog is most likely going to be the time zone that you reside in. This will set the time on your posts to the local time so that you are able to see when your posts do the best so that you can post around that time every time you post.

How your date and time are formatted is going to be a personal choice. There are many different options as to how these will appear and it is up to you to pick how you want them to appear on your blog.

Step four: the theme that you pick is going to say a lot about what your readers can expect from your blog. To change the theme, you are going to click on the appearance menu that is located on the dashboard so that you can see the themes that are available to you. Some of the themes are going to be free while others you will have to purchase.

Step five: if you do not like how the theme is set up, you can customize the theme so that it is how you want it to loo. This is going to be where you change the header images, backgrounds, and colors of the theme.

Step six: the widgets are just the tools that you can add to so that you can connect to other sources. When you go to the appearance menu, you are going to be able to install the widgets that you want and select where on your blog you want them to go. Whenever you click on the arrow button that appears next to it, the configuration options are going to open for you to further customize the widget.

Step seven: going back to your dashboard, you are going to go to posts and add a new post. This is going to be your test post that will enable you to see what it is going to look like on your blog.

When you are creating the post, be sure to give it a title that is going to capture your reader's attention causing them to want to read it further. Also, it is a good idea to write a welcome post so that you can invite your readers to follow along with your blog.

Hosting your own WordPress blog

Step one: if you want to host your own WordPress blog, you are going to have to download WordPress to the web host that you are using so that you can have complete control of your blog. Downloading the software for WordPress is going to be completely free and if you decide to run ads on your blog, you are going to get the money from them.

Step two: there are some hosts that are not going to support a WordPress blog. So, if the host that you are currently using is one of those, you are going to have to choose a different one. There are a few web hosts that you can find that are going to have WordPress already installed or make the installation of it simple for you. A few of the web hosts that you can look at are Go Daddy, HostGator, and DreamHost.

Step three: once you have selected your web host, you are going to need to log into the control panel. This control panel is where you are going to be running everything that needs to be run when it comes to your website.

Step four: this is the step where you will be required to install the script for WordPress. Like mentioned above, many web hosts already have WordPress already installed, all you will need to do is scroll down and locate the installation link that is associated with WordPress.

After it has been installed, you are going to be prompted to create a username and password as the admin for your blog.

Step five: in the event that your web host does not offer WordPress already installed, you will need to go to the WordPress website and download the script for your site.

First you will need to connect to an FTP so that the file from WordPress takes root in the domain that you want it to. Should you want it in a subdomain, you will need to create a folder for that domain and then place the files form WordPress into it.

From here you should open up a web page to upload the files. There is going to be an option that will allow you to run the script installation package, simply click on that link it is going to install itself to your blog.

Step six: now you can log into your blog. You will need to log in using the administrator information that you were asked to provide in an earlier step. Once you have logged in, you will see your dashboard so that you can control anything on your blog.

Step seven: after you have customized your site as you want it to be, create your first post! This post should be your welcome post where you introduce yourself and tell your readers a little about what they can expect from your blog. This post is going to be the post that helps to draw readers to your blog before you truly get into the meat of what you have chosen to write about.

Chapter Five: Publishing Schedules

Once your website has been created successfully, the final major hurdle that you are going to need to overcome is getting into the habit of creating the right types of content at the right time. Consider the following tips when it comes to getting yourself into the proper publishing mindset and remember, it is always better to err on the side of too much, rather than too little new content.

Set goals: If you are not used to writing in large doses on a regular basis, you might find it difficult at first to come up with enough ideas to fill a week's worth of blogs, much less actually write them. Regardless of where your current skill level is at, you will find that setting the right types of goals not only makes it easier for you to write on a regular basis but it will improve your habits as well. When it comes to setting personal goals, it is important that you ensure they are SMART goals if you hope to see the best results.

Specific: SMART goals are specific which means that they have clearly defined points of success and failure. For example, if you set a goal to simply write regularly, then you will likely be unable to follow through, simply because you don't have any way of determining when you have succeeded at your goal and when you have failed. Instead, it is best to set goals related to precisely how many posts you are going to create in a given time period so you will be able to more easily stay on track throughout the process.

Measurable: In addition to being specific, you are going to want to choose goals that are measurable so that you can see how well you are doing over a prolonged period of time. This means that you are going to want to set goals for both the short term as well as the long term so that you have an overall idea of the progress you are making as you work through the individual steps. This means that you will want to set weekly goals as well as larger goals that you can strive for in the long term.

Achievable: While setting goals that are outside the realm of possibility might seem like a good way to motivate yourself, the fact of the matter is that goals that are achievable, if only just, are going to be much more motivating in the long term. On the other hand, it is important that the goal you choose to pursue isn't too easy, as if you feel as though you don't have to try, you will find it much more difficult to get started each day.

Realistic: In addition to being achievable, it is important that the goals you choose are realistic based on the other commitments in your life. Setting goals that are achievable, but not realistic will only set you up for failure in the long term, which will then make it more difficult for you to succeed in the long term.

Timely: Perhaps most important for your purposes at the moment, it is important that any goals you set have an end date that is appropriate to your broader goals associated with your blog. Only by setting firm deadlines will you find the motivation you need in order to see them through to completion.

Meeting your blogging schedule: Before you are able to truly meet your schedule, you have to get your resources together so that you are making it easier for you to publish more content for your readers. When you are blogging, you are going to have to focus on your writing, the design of your post, publishing it, and finally promoting it through the proper channels. Each one of these steps is going to take time and it is important to figure out a process that works for you to ensure you can do it on a daily basis, not just for now but, for the long term.

Finding ideas: The best ways to go about finding ideas for your blog is going to depend on how in tune you are with your niche in general. If you aren't living your life in such a way that you will be able to realistically expect inspiration to strike when you are out and about, then you are going to need to do everything in your power to ensure that your well of inspiration never runs dry. First and foremost, you are going to want to look into news sites that are related to the topic that you are writing about. Up to the minute posts will not only make it seem as though you have your finger on the pulse of your niche but they are practically guaranteed click bait as well which means you can expect new viewers to find your site because of them.

If you find that you are having a hard time reliably coming up with content, odds are you need to do more research on your target niche. Get to know the people you are marketing to, understand how they think, feel and act and you will find that you suddenly have more ideas than you know what to do with.

Creating posts: Now that you know all of how you can create a schedule for posting, you will now be up to where you will be creating the posts that people will be reading. You will need to think of the time that it will take for every post to be set up along with how long those posts are going to be. Then, how long will it take for a graphic to be created should a graphic need to be placed in the post. Lastly, once the post has been published, the promotion process will come into play of where you are going to promote your posts and how you are going to get it out to everyone.

Some blogs actually have a feature that is going to allow you to write a post and have it publish on its own at a particular date and time. This is going to be helpful to keep to your blogging schedule in the event that you find yourself having to step away from your writing for reasons that may be planned or otherwise. If you have this feature with your host, then take advantage of it because you are going to be able to deliver posts on a regular basis without having to worry.

Chapter Six: Monetizing Your Blog

Once you have successfully created your website, all that is left to do is to start actively monetizing it in as many different ways as possible. It is important to keep your expectations realistic at this point and to remember that just as starting your blog was lots of work, so too will be monetizing it. The end results are well worth it, however, and if you persevere then passive income awaits.

Additionally, you need to be aware that getting a full-time paycheck from a blog at this point is going to be a full-time job. Each new post that you create takes you one step closer to a passive income stream, however, so slow and steady wins the race. Early on it is crucial for your blog to have plenty of new content on a regular basis, not just constant advertising. You need to build your readers trust first before you start trying to make money.

Create the right type of content: When it comes to successfully monetizing your blog, the first thing that you are going to need to do is create the type of content that your niche or sub niche is truly going to be interested in. If you are already very active in the niche in question then this should be relatively easy, otherwise you will want to start by doing research into the most popular blogs on the topic as a way of learning not just what those who are interested in the topic are most passionate about, but also learning how they express themselves, what types of slang and jargon they use and the types of things that are important to them both personally and in the workplace. Additionally, spending plenty of time on these sites will provide you with the opportunity to look for gaps in their coverage that you will then be able to exploit on your site.

Once you know what type of content that you should be providing, the next thing you will need to consider is how you will put a personal spin on it. Regurgitating common information will get you nowhere which is why you are going to need to create a niche specific persona if you aren't naturally a person your niche would turn to for advice. This persona shouldn't be a stereotype, but at the same time needs to be someone that a large portion of your audience will relate to. Once your audience can relate to you, you will find that it is much easier to sell them things.

Finally, once you know what you are going to write about, and what slant you are going to put on things, all that is left to do is to get writing. Once your site goes live you are going to want to post multiple pieces of new content every day to ensure that you force people to get in the habit of checking your site regularly which means you are going to need a log of 50 blog posts or so to ensure you have time to keep up the flow. While this might seem high, if you post three times a week it will only last you two weeks. If that seems like too much writing, you might want to reconsider your passive income choice.

Start with monetization basics: No matter what platform you use, you will have the ability to sell ad space. Normally you are going to be able to get a few pennies every time that someone clicks on an ad and the most popular way is to enroll with Google Adsense so that relevant ads are placed without you having to go out and find individual advertisers. Depending on the amount of traffic that your site sees, you could be getting up to $0.50 every time someone clicks on the ad.

Ads are going to be the easiest way for you to make money on your site, but they require lots of page views to truly be profitable on their own. The best way to increase your revenue stream right off of the bat is by joining what is known as an affiliate marketing program that is going to allow you to have a more targeted form of advertising. The most common affiliate advertiser is Amazon and anyone can sign up to be an Amazon affiliate. Once you sign up, all you need to do is to choose products that your niche is interested in, write positive reviews of the products and include a special link that will be provided to you to let your readers buy the product if they are so inclined. Each purchase that is made from your link puts money directly into your pocket in an amount that is proportional to the cost of the item in question.

If you plan on going down this route it is important to only choose products that you have first purchased and can genuinely vouch for. As a blogger, all you have is your name and your reputation and if you tarnish that reputation by shilling cheap products then you will lose readers faster than you can possibly imagine. Likewise, it is important that these types of product reviews are only one of the types of content that you provide if you want people to stick around in the long term. A ratio of 10 percent advertising based posted is typically considered acceptable by many bloggers.

Paid Content: If you regularly offer useful information on your blog, then paid content is a good method for you to consider, especially should the information that you are putting out there help your readers make money. To proceed down this path, all you need to do is make a separate, members only section of your site that allows paid access to various types of content.

- eBooks: you can put all of your top tips or put something new altogether in an ebook, and it will be a reader-friendly way to not only get your content offline but package that content.

- White papers: these are similar to ebooks but they are going to be smaller and more technically written.

- Phone calls: if you are offering a service, phone calls are a good way to sell that advice, have your readers pay for the phone call and any other consulting you may be offering.

- Miniguides: Short guide can be a helpful series that you can sell to your readers on how they can do things.

- Tutorials: Video tutorials can be comprised of the same material as the guides, and you will have the ability to compile tutorials together on what you are an expert at.

- Podcasts may be a rare gift to your readers, and if you have a loyal reader base, they may be willing to pay to be able to hear additional advice, that you have to offer, or just to be able to keep up with your blog whenever they are on the go.

- Videos, another extra, some readers will be willing to pay for it because it makes it easier for them to read your blog without having to stare at your blog and read the words.

Begging

No one likes begging, but no one likes someone who is being sneaky either, so be upfront about wanting to earn money with your blog. But, be polite when you are asking. The people that actually value what you are writing about are going to be more willing to show their support in order to help you keep going and be successful.

- PayPal: PayPal offers a button that you can put on your blog that is going to allow your readers to give you donations.
- Amazon Honor System: this is similar to PayPal's donation button, but it is through Amazon.
- Patreon: with patreon you are going to be using a platform that is based on crowd funding. By using patreon you can get donations for your posts on a regular basis or per post if you prefer. Using patreon, you are going to be able to get monthly donations as well as set a monthly goal.
- Tangible objects: some readers want to give gifts that they made to their favorite people. For people to be able to do this, set up a PO Box that is dedicated to letters and anything else that people may want to send you.

RSS Ads:

For more specialized advertising, RSS is going to allow bloggers to monetize their feeds. But, remember that readers do not want to see their favorite blog overtaken by ads, regular or RSS. So, be sure to limit the amount of RSS ads that are on your blog.

- Pheedo Inc: this RSS platform offers an interactive trigger as well as video options.

- Feedvertising: this is part of text link ads that will be embedded in the RSS feed.

- CrispAds is going to focus the ad network so that you are able to place the ads into entries that are going to show up on your site as well as the feeds.

- FeedBurner Inc: the ads are going to be embedded in the RSS feed while featuring high-quality advertisers such as Best Buy.

- FeddM8: your blog is going to be mobile ready while having the relevant mobile advertising embedded.

Chapter Seven: Promoting Your Blog

When it comes to monetizing your blog, it doesn't matter if you have all of the most interesting content possible as well as the perfect set of ads for your niche, if no one knows about your site then it is all for naught. As such, once you have a decent amount of content built up, the next thing you will need to do is start to get the word out to the world about just what it is you are up to. This is where the persona that you have created comes into play as it will help you create the type of story that other people are interested in following.

The fact of the matter is that blogs are a dime a dozen, which means that yours is going to need to bring something unique to the table if it is going to survive. A major part of that uniqueness is you, which means you will be promoting your persona as much as your blog itself throughout this chapter and the next.

Frequent posts: While this was already touched upon once, it bears repeating here as well. The more individual posts you create each and every day, the easier that it will be for new people to find your blog from a blind search engine search and the more times you will show up on individual pages, giving you an air of credibility to boot. Additionally, it is important to keep in mind that each and everyone one of your posts should include plenty of niche specific keywords and phrases. This will ensure that your posts are indexed to as many different searches as possible which means you are broadening your reach with every new post.

Linking: These days it is becoming increasingly common for Google to give preferential treatment to blogs that are linked to, and link to, other high quality sources. In order to take advantage of this fact, you can start by regularly linking to other reputable blogs in the posts that you create. Additionally, you want to ensure that you have plenty of links to different posts of your own within each post. This interconnecting web of links makes it easier for your site to be indexed by Google which naturally improves your search ranking, making it easier for strangers to stumble upon your site with little prompting. Finally, after your blog has gained some legitimacy, you can reach out to other blogs and offer a link exchange program. Be careful who you get into bed with, however, as it is important to only choose high quality partners if you don't want to process to backfire.

Email signature: When you send out emails to your email list, they are already going to know your blog's URL. But, you email more people than just your blog contacts. Attract the attention of those that do not know that you have a blog so that you can promote your blog and get your name out there. While it might seem like a little thing, an email signature with a link to your blog can be thought of a little like a direct mail campaign. Even if only 5 percent of everyone you email clicks on your link, each one of those is still money in your pocket that you would otherwise leave sitting on the table.

Business cards: Do not just depend on electronic methods of promotion either. When you talk to people and let them know that you own a blog, they are going to want to know your URL and sometimes writing it down is a little bit daunting, and remembering it is never going to happen, so create a business card that is going to contain your URL and your contact information. While this might seem like a fringe scenario, 1,000 business cards will rarely set you back more than $50 and it can be thought of in the same way as your email signature, each individual pageview is a win.

Guerilla marketing: While all of the above are important in order to attract a wider audience, when it comes to building your core niche base you are going to want to seek them out directly where they live. This means you are going to want to seek out the most popular websites related to your niche or sub niche and then make sure that everywhere individual readers turn they see your name. This means you are going to want to become an active member of the forum and comment on everything that is posted. These posts can't just be ads for your blog either, they need to be insightful and useful, this is the only way that you will get people to go outside of their comfort zone and see where all of the good information is coming from.

Additionally, if you followed the advice above and started forming relationships with other blogs then you are going to want to take that relationship to the next level and offer to write guest content in addition to just sharing links. Seeing your name on another site will go a long way towards legitimizing it in the eyes of your niche, and the link that is included at the end of your guest blog will be worth its length in gold assuming, of course, that you manage to provide lots of quality content in the bargain.

Chapter Eight: Social Media and Blogging

Whenever you are trying to build a bigger audience, social media is going to be a natural choice. It is also an exceedingly obvious one which is why your social media game is going to need to be on point if you hope for this approach to be effective in drawing new readers to your blog. Many social media sites provide a blogger with the proper amount of opportunities to gather in new readers while staying in touch with their regular readers. However, if you are only using social media for fun, it tends to get a little overwhelming. In this chapter, you'll learn how to navigate through the complicated maze of social media and still have the proper amount of time to write quality content.

Display social media icons towards the top of the page: Make it simple for your readers to be able to connect with you on all of your social media platforms. When they have to hunt around to try and find where they can connect with you, then they are most likely just going to give up and move on instead. There should be buttons on your page that are going to take them to your Facebook or Twitter with a simple click it should be in the same place on every single one of your pages, period. Additionally, you are going to want your blog's Facebook page to be set up to automatically send out a post each time you create new content which will allow your followers to never miss a chance to give you page views.

StumbleUpon: StumbleUpon acts like an alternate browser that allows users to click through the various pages that their friends and the site have recommended for them based on their stated interests and browser histories. When you submit your blog posts to the system, you are going to be able to share them with people on StumbleUpon and accept their shares back as well, adding your content to a social web of links that can be extremely effective at reaching viewers who otherwise might never view your site. Just like any other social media platform, you will need a strong following in order to get the proper results, however; luckily, people are still trying to figure out how StumbleUpon works so there is still room to build a vibrant and robust following.

RSS feed into LinkedIn profiles: Whenever your blog consists of your professional goals, achievements, or anything job related you should place it on your LinkedIn profile. You can put it under one of the three websites that you are allowed to put on your profile under "blog." However, using the blog application is going to mean that your most recent posts are going to be placed on your profile, so be sure to keep your posts on topic and professional in order for this tactic to be successful.

Pinterest: By "pinning" your best photo onto a themed board, you are going to be able to place a link with the picture that will take the reader to the appropriate blog post. If your blog has a strong presence in visual content such as food, crafts, travel, so on and so forth, you are going to do well on Pinterest since it is all about pictures. Just do not forget to add the Pin it button to your blog so that readers are able to share your content to their boards.

Shorter links: Twitter is going to automatically shorten any links you post so that it does not take up the entire word count that you are allowed when creating a post. But, this is not going to matter on Google+ or Facebook. However, when a link is shortened, you are going to be able to get more access to metrics which are going to tell you how many people have clicked on the link and what time they clicked on the link. With this data, you are going to be able to see the different ways that you can use your content to tantalize your readers and what times you need to be posting in order to see the best results.

Make your username as your blog name: To better promote your blog, you should always use your blog name in things like your Twitter handle, your Pinterest name, your StumbleUpon name and anywhere else you can. This is all an opportunity to gain mind share and whenever people are not wondering about the blog's name, they are going to be able to find you easier on the multiple platforms you may be on this is crucial when it comes to making sure that you are able to develop your online community as easily as possible.

Blogger groups on Facebook: On Facebook, you are going to be able to find some groups that are active and contain valuable resources for any issues you may encounter directly related to your niche. These groups will also be invaluable when it comes to problem-solving any issues you may have while also bringing in more readers to your page because bloggers like to read other blogs related to their niche.

Be generous: Once you have found a blogger community you are going to want to share the love and mention the other niche blogs in your own post as many times they will then return the favor. This sort of cross promotion costs you nothing while at the same time puts new eyes on your content thanks to the reciprocity and is something you should do regularly.

Chapter Nine: Email Marketing

Email is an integral part of everyone's life. With phones in everybody's pocket, emails are received a lot quicker than they used to be so people can easily pop open their phones and see what it is that they have gotten. With emails being so big, it is only smart to think that you should turn your blog followers into email blast followers as well.

You emails can be different than your posts on your blog and that is why you are going to want to have as many followers as possible. Emails are a way that you are going to be getting more followers because when you send out an email that contains stuff that someone wants to share with their friends or family, they are going to forward it and then you are going to get more followers.

Email marketing is going to be effective because you are going to be able to get a high reach of people from those who subscribe to your emails. It is easier to search for an email instead of trying to search through thousands of daily updates on a social media feed to find something that you wanted to read later.

Emails are going to offer some flexibility because it works with any business that you are associated with. When you use the proper email strategies you are going to be able to pull in more customers. Not just that, but you will be able to promote anything that you want that is going to be related to your business. You will not be limited to just your sales pages.

There is going to be less of a risk when you use email marketing because you are not spending money on advertising campaigns that may or may not work. Email marketing is going to carry a lower budget and work just as well. While advertising is going to bring in its fair share of people, it is going to be cheaper to use emails than to worry about putting advertisements up in the proper places.

Unlike other strategies, email marketing has very little that you have to learn in order to place it in your bag of tricks. You are going to get different results depending on what tactic you are using. It is also going to help improve your results. You are bound to make some mistakes, but you will not be wasting your time in learning how to use email marketing.

Unlike with advertisements, you are going to be in full control of what is placed in the emails that you send out. There are not going to be any policy changes that you will have to keep up with because you are the one setting the policies for the emails that come out. There are still some rules that you are going to have to follow when it comes to email marketing, but it is mostly up to you to figure out how you are going to benefit from email marketing. You are not going to have to worry about the rules changing and even if they do change, there will not be a major change to them like what can happen with policies of different web pages.

Personalization

Whenever writing an email, it is easy to fall into the ways that we were taught in addressing it to a specific person. However, when you personalize the email, it is not having the desired effect, a study actually shows that personalization can be harmful to the sender as well as the recipient.

As a business, it is important that you gain the trust of your readers before you jump into being familiar with them. If you are too familiar with them before you have their trust, it is going to come across as strange and most likely get the reader to delete your email without bothering to read it.

Whenever you fake familiarity with your subscribers, it is going to drive them off. But, you do not have to swear off all personalization forms. Whenever you stick to a particular brand of personalization, you are going to earn the trust of your readers quicker.

Personalization should be done in a meaningful way and sparingly. You should have a good knowledge and relationship with your reader before you can enter their name into an email heading.

Subject lines

Your subject line should be short, simple, and to the point. If you create a subject line that is between sixty to seventy characters, you may end up getting more deletes from your subscribers than those who are opening it to read it.

Subject lines that are seventy or more characters have been shown to engage a reader just enough that they want to click on the email and go through the content to see what it is about. At the same rate, subject lines that have forty-nine or less characters are also going to be opened by your readers.

The honest truth is that if your subject line is ten characters or less, you are going to get a reader to open your email faster than if you have a long subject line that is detailing everything that can be put into the body of the email.

In fact, whenever a subject line is short and simple, more people are going to open it because they want to see what the email contains. Subject lines like "hey" or "wow" are going to grab a reader's attention and draw them in because of their curiosity.

In short, long subject lines are going to get you click throughs and short subject lines are going to get your emails opened. It is up to you on which strategy you decide to use, but it is best that you try to avoid the sixty to seventy zone.

Prime time

Even though people have access to their emails almost every hour throughout the day, most people do not check their personal emails during business hours. If you figure that a majority of people work 9 to 5 and then have to take care of their families and make sure they eat and get their kids off to bed, then by the time they are sitting down to do what they want, it is probably around 8 or later.

With this being said, anywhere from 8 to midnight is going to be the opportune time for people to see your email and open it. Another reason that it is a smart idea to send your email later in the day is because when there are less emails coming into someone's inbox, they are going to slow down and read what each email is and who it is coming from instead of mass deleting it.

Mobile

Since most people access their email through a mobile device, you need to ensure that your emails can be seen on a mobile device. If they cannot then you are going to end up losing people and potential profits.

For an email to be readable on a mobile device it should have a majority of the tappable objects in the middle of the screen so that they are not accidentally being clicked on. Your email should also take up one column instead of several like it would on a laptop. Multiple columns makes it harder for a reader to read on their mobile device and most times these emails are discarded. Call to action buttons should be easy to find and select. You should also make the font bigger so it can be read without the need to zoom.

Email over social media

Social media is mostly used for keeping in touch with friends and family while email is used for business and your blog is a business. It may seem as though social media is taking over and that if you are not on social media, then you are going to lose users. But, this is not true.

A study done by SocialTwist shows that out of all the referrals they got that month, over half of them were brought in because of an email that was sent out while the remaining were brought in by two different social media outlets.

Social media has its place, but ultimately, email is better than social media by a long shot.

Weekends

Since most people do not work on the weekends, they are going to be more apt to check their emails since they are not worrying about getting ready for work the next day. This is because a lot of emails are not sent out on the weekends and therefore there are not going to be a massive amount of emails that will need to be deleted perhaps accidentally causing yours to be deleted as well.

Re-engage

You may have a large email list, but how many of those people are actually reading your emails? There may be a lot more people that are inactive on your list then you may realize. Looking at the research, it has been discovered that about sixty-three percent of any subscription list is inactive!

You usually have about the first ninety days after someone signs up for emails from you to get them interested and keep them active in your emails. If you have inactive people on your list, you have to get them re-interested in your emails again. A good place to start is going to be a re-engagement campaign.

To get people reinterested in your blog, you should send out an email with a subject line that is going to grab their attention and then go into possibly explaining how things have changed or might change on your blog.

There is no guarantee that you are going to get them to re-engage in your blog once more. But, it is always worth a try!

Chapter Ten: Blogging Tips

It does not matter if you have been blogging for years or are just starting out, there is always something new to learn when it comes to attracting as many new readers as possible as regularly as possible.

Always create original work: While early on you may find it difficult to come up with enough content to fill a week's worth of blog posts, it is important to never give into the urge to copy a topic that someone else has created. The internet has a very long memory and is great at comparing things to other things. No matter how crafty you think you are being, someone will notice what you are doing and take you to task for it. This will be the death knell for your blog, make no mistake, always create everything you use whole cloth.

Be truthful: Whatever you do, it is important to keep a strong focus on being truthful to your readers. Putting your integrity first means that when you do put your seal of approval on a product people are more likely to listen.

Be awesome: There are plenty of mediocre blogs in the world, if you hope to rise beyond a few hundred page views a month you are going to need to go out of your way to better than average at all times.

Don't expect too much too soon: Especially if you don't do much writing on a regular basis, and even if you do, it can take some time to develop your own unique voice. It is important to not rush this process and to instead let it develop naturally over time. Remember, greatness cannot be rushed.

Pick a theme: Once you start writing and gathering a following, you will not be able to change up your topic or overall approach very much without alienating your existing audience so you need to be locked in before you really get going. Regardless, you should know that your readers are not going to stick around because of what you picked to write about, even though that is how they found your blog. Instead, they are going to stick around because of how you are presenting your topic.

Do not measure your stats too early: If you are only a couple months into your blogging career, the truth of the matter is that it is way too early to be worried about the number of people that visit your blog on a daily basis. It can often take as much as a year before you are fully able to see the trends in people who visit your blog and what types of content they like and dislike. Once you start seeing some real traffic, Google Analytics is a great way to see any trends as they emerge.

Easy to share: Most of the content that is found online is going to be shared through social media. You want your readers to easily be able to tell their loved ones about what you have posted so that maybe you get some more traffic on your blog. Not only does this mean having embedded social media options, it means creating content that can easily be distilled down into a few lines while still be complex enough to warrant passing on.

Encourage a community: Right from your very first post you are going to want to do everything in your power to interact with the community that is springing up around your blog. Engage with every comment, positive or negative, talk to your followers on social media directly, do everything you can to make the people who read your blog feel as though they know you and they will be more likely to listen when you create an affiliate post.

Evergreen content: When it comes to eventually creating a blog with an eye towards a long term passive income stream, it is important to consider as many topics that will be as relevant five years from now as they are today as possible. The more content that you create that will always remain relevant the more pageviews will roll in even when your time as a blogger begins to wind down.

Word count: Attention spans are down today more than ever thanks to the constant demand for attention from 100 different directions that everyone must deal with at all times. To compensate for this fact, it is important you keep you blog short and sweet, while at the same time retaining as much relevant content as possible. A good rule of thumb is the second you find yourself essentially filling space then it is time to wrap things up.

Conviction: If you are writing about something that requires you to pick a side, pick a side and be bold about it. If you turn out to be wrong later on down the road, do not be afraid to admit to it. As a blogger, being right is not nearly as important as speaking with conviction.

Get ideas from your readers: When a reader asks you a question, create a post so that you are interacting with them. This is going to be a great way to tailor your blog to those who are reading it and want to see your blog grow, the same goes for Facebook posts or tweets.

Understand your audience: Understanding your audience is going to better help them understand themselves. There is going to be a lot of upfront research involved, but it is going to pay off in the long run. Understanding is going to mean that you have a better idea of what you should post so that it resonates with your readers. A good way to do this is to ask your readers on social media. Should people respond well to it, then it is probably a topic that you are going to be able to write about.

Write for yourself: First and foremost, you need to write for yourself. Forget that others are going to be reading what you write, and just put your thoughts out there. Write it out, and readers will come. Not everyone is going to like what you have to say, but then again you don't need to worry about pleasing everyone just your core audience. Writing for yourself is also going to make a difference in your blog. You may end up publishing more because you are not posting based on the reception of what you posted, but instead, you are posting whenever you have something to say.

Love the readers that already exist on your site: Some bloggers end up becoming so obsessed with finding new readers that they tend to forget about the users that they already have. Yes, you want new users, but that does mean that you can forget the ones that are already faithful. Show them that you value them for what they have done to help your blog grow. Look at your blog as a promise to your readers. They want a blog that is going to give them real content that is going to match their needs. It is sort of like a newspaper that someone is expecting to be delivered every day. Do not just give them junk that they can get anywhere; they are loyal to you, and they came to your blog for a reason. So, give them what they have been getting from you the entire time.

Focus on building an amazing call to action: You may see that some of your posts do well while others do not. You may even have very few people following you on Facebook or Twitter. Do not make your readers work to find your accounts. Do the work for them and do not place it in the sidebar because it will be looked over thanks to ads often being put in the sidebar. Whenever you finish up a post, add in a call to action button so that they have the ability to sign up for your emails or follow you on social media. You are going to see an increase in followers very quickly.

Be true to your voice: People are not going to follow you because of your site; they need to follow you because they care about you. Your voice is important, but it is sometimes overlooked. If you do not know how your own writing voice sounds, the more you write, the easier it is going to be for you to find out where your voice lies. You can write about whatever you want, but what matters is that it resonates with your readers. Focus on how you are saying things, not what you are saying.

Catchy headlines: It does not matter how great your content is, you need to have headlines that catch reader's attention. It only takes a single second for someone to decide if they are going to read your post based on your headline. The headline needs to be desirable for people so that they are motivated to share your post. Keep headlines simple, useful, bold, and powerful. In that second that it takes for your reader to choose to read what you have written or not, you have to be able to draw them in. It is not always going to be easy, but if you work at it, then you are going to have the ability to create the proper headline.

Make it worth referencing: Anyone can cite you at any given time for any given reason. But, it is going to leave you with fascinating ideas or findings, you want your posts to reflect this. You should not rely solely on research, but make sure that each post is original so that it can be citable on the web elsewhere.

Conclusion

Thank for making it through to the end of *Blogging Business*, I hope it was informative and able to provide you with all of the tools you need to achieve your goals whatever it may be.

The next step is to begin the research that you need to do in order to find your blog niche. Once you have done that, you are ready to move on to the next step of starting your blog.

Be sure to weigh the pros and cons of everything that you research so that you are not starting a blog that is going to end up failing in the end. Also, remember that you should not worry about money when you are first starting out. Worry about getting your daily views up so that you have a solid reader base before you begin to worry about money.

With a blog, you are going to have more freedoms than if you were to work a regular job. It may not be for everyone because it is going to require patience and if you do not have it, then this is not the business for you. Should you decide that this is something that you want to peruse, good luck!

Finally, if you found this book useful in any way, a review is always appreciated!

www.ingramcontent.com/pod-product-compliance
Lightning Source LLC
Chambersburg PA
CBHW061449180526
45170CB00004B/1625